Cherry-Blossoms

JAPANESE HAIKU
SERIES III

TRANSLATIONS OF
POEMS BY BASHO·
BUSON·ISSA·SHIKI
AND OTHERS

THE PETER
PAUPER PRESS

MOUNT VERNON · NEW YORK

A NOTE ON THIS BOOK OF HAIKU

In Japan cherry-blossoms are a favorite subject of paintings and poems, and are indeed a symbol to the Japanese people of the transitory delight of the "floating world" — as they have called this life on earth. For cherry-blossoms last only three days, and the Buddhist Japanese thinks of his own life as an equally brief flowering in the endless cycle of reincarnation and dissolution.

Because the *haiku* is a poem only seventeen syllables long, and is usually a brief poignant insight into the universality of this endless cycle, the title *Cherry-Blossoms* has been given to this our third collection of *haiku* translations.

Japanese poets of the present continue to write *haiku*: Harold G. Henderson has estimated that perhaps a million new *haiku* are published commercially in magazines each year. But the present collection is taken from the famous poets of the past. Thus the reader will find the names Basho, Buson, Issa and Shiki much in evidence, for these four are the greatest practitioners. A few facts about these men, and a discussion of the difficulties of *haiku* translation, are to be found in our two previous collections.

Here it is necessary only to remind the reader that the poems are not intended to be clear statements. They are fleeting responses or impressions which usually illuminate the poet's awareness — and our own — of the identity of life on different planes. It is the Buddhist doctrine (and most of these poets are Zen Buddhists) that all things and creatures in this world are temporary manifestations risen from the eternal, infinite ocean of Life; and that everything, — from a mountain peak to a cherry-blossom, from a beautiful girl to the little excrement of a bird, — is a part of the universal and inter-related brotherhood of creation.

Of course, not all these poems have this subtle quality. There are a number purely humorous or descriptive.

The *haiku* almost always has a season key-word. Here these have often been omitted, but the poems are arranged by seasons. Since the New Year traditionally begins the Spring, a few cold poems start the book; but the snow soon melts and leaves and blossoms appear.

The interested reader is referred to our *Japanese Haiku*: Series I, *The Four Seasons*, Haiku Series II, and *Haiku Harvest*, Series IV.

Cherry-Blossoms

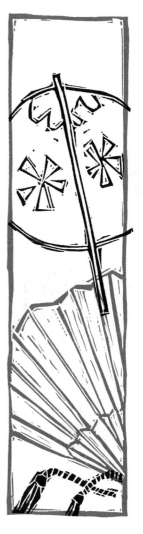

DECORATIONS AND
LETTERING BY
JEFF HILL

Spring

NEW YEAR'S EVE

I CAN SNORE IN PEACE . . .
   THE NEW YEAR
     WON'T CONFRONT ME
TILL TOMORROW NOON
           BUSON

NEW YEAR'S DAY . . . POET
   THOUGH I BE
     I'LL PROUDLY WEAR
MY FATHER'S SCABBARD
           KYORAI

IN THE NEW YEAR DAWN
   SOLEMN AND
     DELIBERATE
TALL CRANES GO MARCHING
           KIKAKU

FROM THE MOUNTAIN PASS
   SEE THE SUNLIT
     CASTLE TOWN . . .
FLYING NEW-YEAR KITES
               TAIGI

SEEING MY BIRTH-CORD
KEPT AT OUR OLD
    NATIVE PLACE . . .
NEW YEAR'S DAY I WEPT
              BASHO

NO YOU DON'T! GET OUT! . . .
   THUS THEY WARMLY
    WELCOMED ME
TO THEIR NEW-YEAR FEAST
             ROTSU

SNOW IS MELTING . . .
   FAR IN THE MISTED
    MOUNTAINS
A CAW-CAWING CROW
            GYODAI

SPRING AT EARLY DAWN . . .
ON THE TIPS OF
BARLEY LEAVES
LITTLE LAST PALE FROST
ONITSURA

UP FROM APRIL SNOW
RISING UDO SPROUTS . . .
TENDER
PURPLE SUCCULENT
BASHO

AT DEAR BASHO'S GRAVE
PALE THIN TRANSIENTS
WE PAUSE . . .
SPRING MIST, SAD PUPIL
JOSO

HEAR THOSE BABY MICE
HUDDLED IN THEIR
NEST . . . PEEPING
TO THE SPARROWLETS
BASHO

8

ABOVE THE HAMLET:
  GREEN THE SILENT
    BAMBOO-GROVE . . .
WHITE LINGERING SNOW
          TAIGI

SPRING COBALT OCEAN . . .
  ACROSS SNOW-WHITE
    MOUNTAINS FLY
BLACK RETURNING BIRDS
          SHIKI

IMMEDIATELY . . .
  ON THEIR SPRING
    RETURN TIRELESS
SWALLOWS ZIG-ZAGGING
          TAIGI

SEE: OUR CANDLELIGHT
  ILLUMINATES
    THE SAPLING'S
FRESH-UNFOLDED GOLD
          BUSON

9

TROOPS OF TOURISTS COME
    FOR APRIL
    FLOWER-VIEWING . . .
OH, THEY'RE SPARROW-MEN
               BASHO

GUSTY SPRING BREEZES . . .
    BUT THE STUBBORN
    PLUM BUDS STILL
GRIPPING THEIR THIN TWIGS
             ONITSURA

SPRING UNFOLDS ANEW . . .
    NOW IN MY SECOND
    CHILDHOOD
FOLLY, FOLLY, TOO
                 ISSA

BONY BRUSHWOOD TWIGS
    CUT DOWN AND STACKED
    IN BUNCHES . . .
YET BRAVELY BUDDING
             BONCHO

PLACING THE KITTEN
   TO WEIGH HER
     ON THE BALANCE ...
SHE WENT ON PLAYING
             ISSA

SPRING EVENING BEACH ...
   HELPING FISHERMEN
   UNLOAD
LIVING SEA-TREASURE
             RANKO

IT IS SPRING AGAIN ...
   GAY IN THE GARDEN
   GATHER
SUN-BATHING SPARROWS
            ONITSURA

TREMENDOUS FORCES ...
   STONE-PILED FENCE
   ALL TUMBLED DOWN
BY TWO CATS IN LOVE
            SHIKI

AFTER THE SHOWER . . .
  SPRING-ENCHANTED
  SPARROW-FOLK
CHATTER ON THE EAVES
                    UKO

SILENT CHERRY-BLOOM . . .
  AGAIN WITH YOUR
  OLD ELOQUENCE
ADDRESS MY INNER EAR
                  ONITSURA

HAVING SCOURED MY SKIN
  AND BOWED MY SKULL
  TO BUDDHA . . .
NOW FOR CHERRY-BLOOM!
                    ISSA

AFTERNOON GARDEN . . .
  PLANTING PERHAPS
  SEVEN SEEDS . . .
I'M CONVALESCENT!
                    SHIKI

THIS BABY . . . EVEN
   WHEN WE SHOW HIM
   CHERRY BUDS . . .
OPENS EAGER LIPS
              SEIFU-JO

MOUNTAIN-TOP OF CLOUDS
   TOWERING BEHIND
   THE HEDGE . . .
OR A FLOWERING PLUM?
              SHIRO

DANCING: THE FOX TREADS
   AMONG THE PALE
   NARCISSI
IN GARDEN MOONLIGHT
              BUSON

AFTER SPRING SUNSET
   MIST RISES FROM
   THE RIVER . . .
SPREADING LIKE A FLOOD
              CHORA

THEN THE PEONIES
    EXTINGUISHING
    ALL OTHERS . . .
OPENED THEIR PETALS
                    KIICHI

ENDLESS MAYTIME RAIN . . .
    SNEAKING BACK ONE
    NIGHT, THE MOON
PERCHED IN THE PINE-TREE
                    RANKO

NOW THAT I AM OLD
    EVEN TENDER DAYS
    OF SPRING
SEE . . . CAN MAKE ME CRY
                    ISSA

BEAUTIFUL LADY
    BUFFETED BY RUDE
    SPRING WINDS . . . WHAT
SWEET STORM YOU MAKE!
                    KITO

ON THE SHINING ROOF
   THE BOY'S ABANDONED
   STRING-BALL
SOAKING UP SPRING RAIN
               BUSON

SWEET SPRING SHOWER . . .
   ENOUGH TO WET
   THE TINY SHELLS
ON THIS LITTLE BEACH
               BUSON

ERE SPRING GUESTS ARRIVE
   WE LIGHT THE
   SUPPER CANDLES
EACH FROM SHINING EACH
               BUSON

DULL-DREARY RAIN-DAY . . .
   DRIPPING PAST
   MY GATE A GIRL
BEARING IRISES
           SHINTOKU

15

YES: THE YOUNG SPARROWS
   IF YOU TREAT THEM
      TENDERLY . . .
THANK YOU WITH DROPPINGS
               ISSA

FOLLOWING THE BANK . .
   FOR MILES NO RIVER-
      SPANNING BRIDGE
THIS LONG SPRING DAY
               SHIKI

AT TAKIGUCHI
   VOICES CALLING
      FOR A LIGHT . . .
DARKENING SPRING RAIN
               BUSON

PATTERING SHOWER . . .
   THEY ARE PUTTING
      OUT THE LAMPS
ALL DOWN DOLL-SHOP LANE
               BUSON

FLOODED PADDY-FIELDS . . .
THE LAKE HAS COME
TO TOWN ALL GREEN
WITH SEEDLING RICE
BAKUSUI

VANISHING SPRINGTIME . . .
WISTFULLY
THE LONELY WIDOW
POUTS AT HER MIRROR
SEIBI

BLOWN CHERRY-BLOSSOMS
FALL AND FLOAT
UPON THE COLD
RICE-PADDY WATERS
KYOROKU

THE GAY WATERWHEEL
IN THE VALLEY
POURS PETALS
FROM MOUNTAIN CHERRIES
CHOGETSU

17

Summer

O SPRINGTIME TWILIGHT . . .
　PRECIOUS MOMENT
　WORTH TO ME
A THOUSAND PIECES

　　　　　SOTOBA

REPLY:

O SUMMER TWILIGHT . . .
　BUG-DEPRECIATED
　TO A
MERE FIVE HUNDRED

　　　　　KIKAKU

BOUNCING BAMBOO DIPPER
　IN THE WATER-TUB . . .
　FOLLOWING
A FLY-AWAY BIRD

　　　　　HORO

A BABY SPARROW ...
    HOPPING
    WITH CURIOSITY
TO WATCH MY BRUSHWORK
                    SHOHA

HOW COOL...SWEET GRASSES
    SCYTHED IN FIELDS
    AT EARLY DAWN
ENTERING OUR GATE
                    BONCHO

ON THE GIDDY SWING ...
    TINY GIRL-CHILD
    CLUTCHING TIGHT
HER SPRAY OF BLOSSOMS
                    ISSA

AH ROADSIDE SCARECROW
    WE'VE HARDLY
    STARTED GABBING ...
AND I HAVE TO GO
                    IZEN

19

PERHAPS THIS VOICELESS
   WANDERER DREAMS
     OF FLOWERS . . .
BUTTERFLY DOZER
            REIKAN

SOMETIMES THE FARMER
   TROTS OUT TO SEE
     HIS SCARECROW . . .
SLOWLY HE WALKS BACK
           BUSON

THAT DARK WATERFOWL
   ALTHOUGH APPEARING
     WEIGHTED . . .
SEE HOW IT CAN FLOAT!
           ONITSURA

AH BOLD NIGHTINGALE . . .
   EVEN BEFORE
     HIS LORDSHIP
YOU WON'T MEND YOUR SONG
           ISSA

THAT FAT OLD BULL-FROG
   SAT THERE STARING
    BACK AT ME
WITH A SOUR FACE

             ISSA

IN FLAT SUNSET LIGHT
   A BUTTERFLY
    WANDERING
DOWN THE CITY STREET

            KIKAKU

SOMEONE IS WALKING
   OVER THE WOODEN
    BRIDGE . . . HEAR
THE DEEP FROG-SILENCE

            RYOTO

A WAGON RUMBLING . . .
   AND OUT FROM
    SILENT GRASSES
A SUDDEN BUTTERFLY

            SHOHA

INTO THE BLINDING
　　SETTING SUN THE
　　SCARECROW STARES . . .
STILL INDIFFERENT

SHIRAO

GAY . . . AFFECTIONATE . . .
　　WHEN I'M REBORN
　　I PRAY TO BE A
WHITE-WING BUTTERFLY

ISSA

SQUATTING LIKE BUDDHA:
　　BUT BITTEN
　　BY MOSQUITOES
IN MY NIRVANA

OEMARU

AT THE ANCIENT SHRINE
　　TARNISHED GOLD-FOIL . . .
　　AND GREEN LEAVES
AWAKENING TIME

CHORA

22

EVEN WITH INSECTS . . .
   SOME ARE HATCHED
   OUT MUSICAL . . .
SOME, ALAS, TONE-DEAF
              ISSA

PLANTED ROWS OF BEANS
   AND RANDOM CLUMPS
   OF LILIES . . .
PROSPEROUS ISLET!
             SHIKI

NIGHTINGALE WEEPING
   AND CEASELESS OCEAN
   MOANING . . .
SOON O SOON THE DAWN
             SHIRAO

IN SUMMER MOONLIGHT . . .
   GLITTERING BROOKLET
   RUNNING
DOWN OUR VILLAGE STREET
             SHIRAO

23

TWO JADE-GREEN HILLTOPS
   STAND IN THEIR
   SUMMER LEAFAGE
MIRROR-IMAGES

              KYORAI

YELLOW FIREFLY...
   LITTLE LAMP-FLAME
   THAT TO THE
HUMAN TOUCH IS CHILL

              SHIKI

SUNNY FIELDS AND WARM...
   SEE THE MONK'S FACE
   PEEPING OUT
FROM THE TEMPLE FENCE

              ISSA

A CRABLET CRAWLING
   UP MY ANKLE-BONE...
   AH COOL
MEANDERING BROOK

              BASHO

IN MY NATIVE PLACE
   THERE'S THIS PLANT:
   AS PLAIN AS GRASS
BUT BLOOMS LIKE HEAVEN
            ISSA

PITIFUL BLIND CHILD . . .
   AND SO BRIEF
   THE ROSE OF SHARON
GARLANDING HER PORCH
            SHIRAO

DAYLIGHT AT THE INN . . .
   THROUGH MY LOOPED
   MOSQUITO NETS
A MORNING-GLORY
            SHIRO

TWILIGHT WATERING . . .
   AND PLEASE,
   A COOLING SPRINKLE
FOR WRENS AND CRICKETS
            KIKAKU

HAVING TUMBLED OFF
   HIS GRASS-BLADE . . .
THE FIREFLY
BUZZES UP AGAIN

                    BASHO

MOONLIGHT NIGHTINGALE
   CASTS A WHISTLING
   LINE OF SOUND
OVER THE MILLPOND

                    BASHO

AS LIGHTNING FLASHES . . .
   ZIG-ZAG SCREECHES
   OF THE HERON
FLYING IN THE DARK

                    BASHO

HEREBY I ASSIGN,
   IN PERPETUITY,
    TO WIT :
TO THIS BIRD THIS FENCE

                    ISSA

STUBBORN WOODPECKER . . .
  STILL HAMMERING
  AT TWILIGHT
AT THAT SINGLE SPOT

      ISSA

AT SILENT NOONTIDE . . .
  FAR ACROSS
  THE FLOWER-FIELDS
HEAR THE SIGHING SEA

      BUSON

HEAR THE HUMMING
  AS HONEYSUCKLE
  PETALS FALL . . .
DISTURBED MOSQUITOS

      BUSON

THE SICKLY ORCHID
  THAT I TENDED SO . . .
  AT LAST
THANKS ME WITH A BUD

      TAIGI

27

POT-IMPRISONED NOW . . .
   PALELY DREAMING
     OCTOPUS
IN SUMMER MOONLIGHT
BASHO

CURLED ON THE FAN . . .
   AHA! I'VE CAUGHT YOU
     TOM-CAT
FAST ASLEEP AGAIN!
ISSA

HIGH SUN STILL BURNING
   IN THE FALCON'S
     EYES . . . DOWN TO
MY EARTH-BOUND WRIST
TAIRA

BUT SEE THE MOUNTAIN . . .
   SHAKING WITH THE
     WAVES OF HEAT
WHERE DAY HAS GONE
ONITSURA

WHAT A MONSTER KITE!
   EVEN THE BRAVEST
   EAGLE
WOULD NOT DARE ATTACK!
              SHIKI

YELLOW BUTTERFLY . . .
   FLUTTERING
   FLUTTERING ON
OVER THE OCEAN
              SHIKI

COOL ON BLUE WATER
   THAT OVERHANGING
   ISLET
WITH ITS PINE ASKEW
              SHIKI

WHAT A COOLING BREEZE!
   NOW ALL STIFLED
   GRASSHOPPERS
   GAILY SING AGAIN
              ISSA

I WILL NOT FORGET
　　THIS LONELY SAVOR
　　OF MY LIFE'S
ONE LITTLE DEWDROP
　　　　　　　BASHO

MOONLIGHT SLANTING
　　THROUGH ALL THIS
　　LONG BAMBOO GROVE . . .
AND NIGHTINGALE SONG
　　　　　　　BASHO

IN THE RAIN-PINKED POND
　　STILL-UNSLAUGHTERED
　　SILLY DUCKS
REJOICE WITH QUACKING
　　　　　　　ISSA

SPARROW FAMILY . . .
　　PLAYING AT HIDE
　　AND SEEK
IN THE TEA-BUSHES
　　　　　　　ISSA

TWILIGHT FLOWER-FIELD . . .
   MOONRISE IN
   THE EASTERN SKY
SUNSET IN THE WEST
            BUSON

NIGHT IS DARKENING . . .
   SILENT IN
   THE PADDY POOL
SHINES THE MILKY WAY
            IZEN

ON THAT INCH OF LAND
   BEANS GREW TO
   OUR VERY DOOR . . .
YET GRAND IN MOONLIGHT!
            ISSA

WITH ME ON THE CLIFF
   ANOTHER POET . . .
   FELLOW-GUEST
OF THE SUMMER MOON
            KYORAI

INQUIRING WREN
   LOOKING HERE AND
   LOOKING THERE . . .
HAVE YOU LOST YOUR BAG?
                ISSA

THE SADNESS OF IT . . .
   UNDER THE
   HERO'S HELMET,
TARNISHED NOW, A CRICKET
               BASHO

TWO WATER-LILIES
   SHINING SERENELY
   GOLDEN . . .
RAINDROP-DIMPLED POOL
               BUSON

WHILE THE BOBOLINK
   SINGS CHEERILY
   HE GIVES MY SHACK
THE COLD CRITIC'S EYE
               ISSA

FLOATING BUTTERFLY
    WHEN YOU DANCE
        BEFORE MY EYES . . .
ISSA, MAN OF MUD

ISSA

SUPERNATURAL
    COOL BREEZE . . .
        BUDDHA'S PARADISE
MUST LIE THATAWAY

ISSA

INSECTS POOR INSECTS . . .
    HOW WISE TO PURGE
        YOUR KARMA
CRYING PENITENCE

OTOKUNI

WE HARK TO CRICKET
    AND TO HUMAN
        CHIRPINGS . . . WITH
EARS SO DIFFERENT

WAFU

33

SLOW HOT SILENT HOURS . . .
  IN THE AFTERNOON
  A PHEASANT
SETTLES ON THE BRIDGE.
                 BUSON

THE SOFT SUMMER MOON . . .
  WHO IS IT MOVES
  IN WHITE THERE . . .
ON THE OTHER BANK?
                 CHORA

AT MY HUT I FEAR
  ALL I CAN REALLY
  TEMPT YOU WITH . . .
SMALLISH MOSQUITOES
                 BASHO

WHILE I SWOOP MY NET,
  DELIBERATE
  BUTTERFLY . . .
YOU NEVER HURRY
                 GARAKU

34

AH . . . MORNING-GLORY
  GLOWING WITH
    THE INDIGO
OF SOME MOUNTAIN
                    BUSON

SILENT THE GARDEN
    WHERE THE
    CAMELLIA-TREE
OPENS ITS WHITENESS
                    ONITSURA

FROM THE DAY IT'S BORN
    OF ABANDONED
    STICKS AND RAGS . . .
ELDERLY SCARECROW
                    NYOFU

NOW THIS GOOD SEA-SLUG
    HAS BOTH HEAD
    AND TAIL . . . BUT GOD
KNOWS WHICH IS WHICH
                    KYORAI

THAT NIGHT WHEN I HAD
SOLD MY LOWER
FIELD . . . I LAY
WAKEFUL FROM FROG-CALLS
HOKUSHI

HEY! WHY DON'T YOU HELP
THAT BUZZING
HORSE-FLY OPEN
THE STICKING SKYLIGHT?
ISSA

DAWN-TWITTERING BIRDS . . .
OUR OVERNIGHT
BIG-CITY GUEST
ALONE IS STIRRING
SHOHA

TENDER BAMBOO-SHOOTS
AND BABY'S TENDER
GUM-PINKS . . .
TINY TOOTH-CUTTING
RANSETSU

36

BOUNCING THE BALL . . .
   SHE BENDS TO MAKE
    A FACE AT HER
MEOWING KITTEN

ISSA

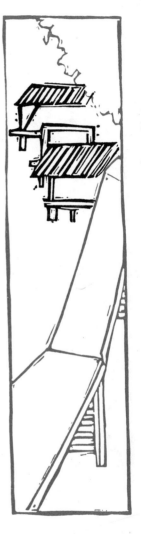

IN THE SUDDEN BURST
  OF SUMMER RAIN . . .
   WIND-BLOWN BIRDS
CLUTCHING AT GRASSES

BUSON

LIKE A BUTTERFLY . . .
   THE PILGRIM'S
    TOMBOY YOUNGSTER
TROTS UNEVENLY

SHIKI

THE MONKS EXHIBIT
   BUDDHA'S IMAGE . . .
    SPARROWS TOO
ARE DAWN-LIGHT LOOKERS

ISSA

Autumn

ON THE EBB-TIDE BEACH
   THE HURRYING CRAB
   STOPS SHORT . . .
THERE IS A FOOTPRINT!
ROFU

BRACED IN THE WATERS . . .
   SCARECROW IN
   THE FLOODED FIELD
GRIMLY ENDURES IT
SHIKI

AH MY FOREST HUT . . .
   WHERE THE FRIENDLY
   WOODPECKER
KNOCKS AT DOOR AND POST
BASHO

ON THIS STILL WATER
   SEE WHERE
   HIS REFLECTION
MEETS THE WATERFOWL
           MAHARA

QUITE THE STUPIDEST
   OF ALL LIVING
   CREATURES IS
A DRY OLD SCARECROW
           SHIKI

AUTUMN NIGHTS ARE COLD...
   CRUSHING THE TINY
   CHILD TO ME ...
WARM LOVELY YOUNGLING
           SHIKI

BEHIND THE TWISTED
   BRANCHES WITH
   THE EAGLE'S NEST ...
RED SINKING SUN-BALL
           BONCHO

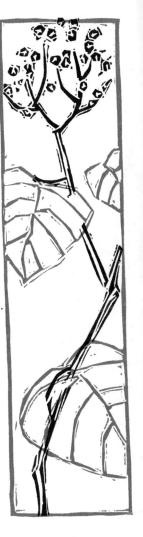

AS I LIGHT THE LAMP
 BEHOLD . . . TO EVERY
 SINGLE DOLL
ITS OWN REAL SHADOW
                          SHIKI

MOTHER LOST, LONG GONE . . .
 AT THE DEEP DARK SEA
 I STARE . . .
AT THE DEEP DARK SEA
                          ISSA

AH SACRED SWALLOW . . .
 TWITTERING OUT
 FROM YOUR NEST IN
GREAT BUDDHA'S NOSTRIL
                          ISSA

TEA-KETTLE HANDLE . . .
 I'LL CUT IT FROM
 THE BAMBOO
OF THAT BUBBLING WREN
                          KIKAKU

WEEPING . . . WILLOWS
    KNEEL HERE BY
      THE WATERSIDE
MINGLING LONG GREEN HAIR
         KYORAI

GATHERING STARLINGS
    CRY AS THEY
      SPRINKLE BERRIES
FROM THE AUTUMN TREE
        SHIKI

SILVERY HERRINGS
    POURING . . .
      A LIVE WATERFALL
FROM NET TO BASKET
        KIKAKU

AH LEAFLESS WILLOW . . .
    BENDING OVER
      THE DRY POOL
OF STRANDED BOULDERS
        BUSON

41

O YOU SNUB-NOSE DOLL!
   MAYBE YOUR
   MOTHER DIDN'T
PINCH AND PULL ENOUGH
                    BUSON

PERCHED ON THE BAMBOO
   MARKER OF A
   NEW-DUG GRAVE . . .
THE WAITING DRAGONFLY
                    KITO

ALL ALONG THE BEACH . . .
   PLOVERS PLAYING
   AT SOME GAME
INVOLVING WET-FOOT
                    BUSON

WITH PHILOSOPHY
   HE CONTEMPLATES
   THE MOUNTAIN . . .
OLD PROFESSOR FROG
                    ISSA

42

AT THE SETTING SUN . . .
   WASHING DOWN
   HIS WEARY HORSE
IN THE AUTUMN SEA
                SHIKI

ON THIS PLAIN OF MIST
   NOTHING BUT FLAT
   ENDLESSNESS . . .
AND RED-RISING SUN
                SHIRO

RISING HARVEST MOON . . .
   FROM THIS HUT
   AS YET UNWALLED
I WILL VIEW IT WELL
                SHIRAO

BITTER BROKEN REEDS . . .
   DAY IN DAY OUT
   THE FALLEN
FLOAT AWAY . . . AFAR
                RANKO

43

PENETRATING HOT
    SEPTEMBER SUN . . .
    ON MY SKIN
FEEL THE COOLING BREEZE
                        BASHO

I AM GROWING OLD . . .
    O SWEET BIRD
    DISAPPEARING
INTO AUTUMN DUSK
                        BASHO

WHO IS THAT, HUDDLED
    IN A STRAW-COAT . . .
    STARING AT OUR
HOLIDAY PARADE?
                        BASHO

SEE THIS DRAGONFLY . . .
    HIS FACE IS
    PRACTICALLY
NOTHING ELSE BUT EYES
                        CHISOKU

44

COMPANION CUCKOO . . .
   KEEP YOUR EYE COCKED
   ON MY HUT
UNTIL I COME BACK

ISSA

REDDISH MORNING SKY . . .
   RAIN FOR YOU TODAY
   I GUESS,
LITTLE LUCKY SNAIL!

ISSA

WITHIN PALE SILENCE
   SPREADING FROM
   EVENING MOONLIGHT . . .
SUDDEN CICADA

HAJIN

WET MORNING GARDEN . . .
   MY SUNNY
   CHRYSANTHEMUMS
ARE SEA-MIST-SHROUDED

SAMPU

WITH THE MOON-RISING . . .
   LEAF AFTER LEAF
   AFTER LEAF
FALLS FLUTTERING DOWN
SHIKI

I DIDN'T ENTER . . .
   BUT I STOPPED
   IN REVERENCE . . .
AUTUMN-LEAF TEMPLE
BUSON

SUDDEN RADIANCE . . .
   AFTER OCTOBER
   RAINSTORM
RE-REDDENED PEPPERS
BUSON

THE PEOPLE, WE KNOW . . .
   BUT THESE DAYS
   EVEN SCARECROWS
DO NOT STAND UPRIGHT
ISSA

46

ONLY WITHERED GRASSES
    IN YOUR CAGE? . . .
    O CRICKET CAPTIVE
MY APOLOGIES!
                    SHOHA

FROM FISH-BOAT TORCHES
    SPARKS ARE FALLING . . .
    POOR TETHERED
SCORCH-FACE CORMORANTS
                    KAKEI

THIS IS MY OWN PLACE . . .
    MUD-HUT AND
    COMPANION TREE
SHEDDING AUTUMN LEAVES
                    CHORA

FROM THE HAUNTED HUT
    SMOKE IS SEEPING
    IN THE RAIN . . .
SOMEONE IS INSIDE!
                    BUSON

47

SEPTEMBER LIGHTNING . . .
   WHITE CALLIGRAPHY
     ON HIGH
SILHOUETTES THE HILL
          JOSO

SEE . . . SIX GAPING BEAKS
   WAITING FOR
     THE MOTHER-BIRD
IN COLD AUTUMN RAIN
          ISSA

SILENT AUTUMN AIR . . .
   HERE AND THERE
     AMONG THE HILLS
RISING THIN BLUE SMOKES
         GYODAI

THE FISHERMAN'S HUT . . .
   WHERE LIVELY CRICKETS
     MINGLE NOW
WITH DRYING SHRIMP
         BASHO

ANNIVERSARY OF DEATH

RISING AUTUMN MOON . . .
   LIGHTING IN MY
   LAP THIS YEAR
NO PALE SICKLY CHILD
               ONITSURA

FOR FALL FESTIVALS
   OUR RELIGIOUS
   DRAGONFLIES
DON RED GARMENTS TOO
               ISSA

WILD GEESE O WILD GEESE
   WERE YOU LITTLE
   FELLOWS TOO . . . WHEN
YOU FLEW FROM HOME?
               ISSA

BY ABANDONED ROADS
   THIS LONELY
   POET MARCHES
INTO AUTUMN DUSK
              BASHO

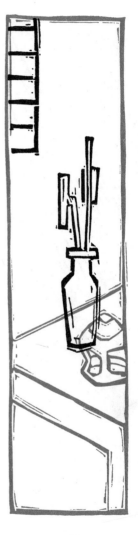

Winter

TELL ME : WHERE DOES THIS
    UNEXPECTED COLD SNAP
    COME FROM . . .
WEATHERWISE SCARECROW?
                ISSA

WINE-DRINKING-WAKEFUL
    ALL ALONE THAT
    BITTER NIGHT
I STARTED AT SNOWFALL
              BASHO

SNOW-ISOLATED . . .
    ONCE MORE I PRESS
    MY BACK AGAINST
MY THINKING-POST
              BASHO

BACK TO MY HOME TOWN
AND BURIAL
IN MY HUT . . .
FIVE COLD FEET OF SNOW

ISSA

WINTER WOODCUTTER . . .
WHEN YOUR AXE CUTS
HOME I SCENT
UNEXPECTED SPRING

BUSON

MY OLD FATHER TOO
LOOKED LONG ON THESE
WHITE MOUNTAINS
THROUGH LONELY WINTERS

ISSA

FEEBLE FEEBLE SUN . . .
IT CAN SCARCELY
STRETCH ACROSS
WINTER-WASTED FIELDS

BAKUSUI

WINTER-SOLITARY . . .
  I FIND SOLACE
  IN THIS OLD
CHINESE-PAINTED PINE
                    BASHO

THE MOURNING FATHER
DEEP UNDER ASHES . . .
  BURNING CHARCOAL
  CHILLED NOW BY
HIS HISSING TEARS
                    BASHO

IN THE RAINY DAWN
  SEE WHERE I CREPT
  OUT OF BED . . .
HOLE IN THE BEDCLOTHES
                    JOSO

A MOUNTAIN HAMLET . . .
  UNDER THE GREAT
  WHITE SNOWDRIFT
A GURGLING BROOK
                    SHIKI

AT FREEZING MIDNIGHT
   HEAR THAT RAT
     GO RUMMAGING . . .
DIRTY KITCHEN DISHES
               BUSON

EVEN MY LAMP-LIGHT . . .
   HIBERNATING
   IN A FROZEN
WINTER-WHITE HALO
            YAHA

LAST NIGHT A SNOWFALL . . .
   TODAY CLEAR COBALT
   HEAVEN AND
WHITE-MANTLED PINES
            ROKA

A BITTER NIGHT . . . BUT
   LONG PRACTICE
   WITH COLD HUNGER
PERMITTED ME TO SLEEP
            IZEN

SOFT SNOWFLAKES SETTLE
  DOWN ON THESE
  UNSTIRRING DUCKS . . .
A WORLD OF SILENCE
                    SHIKI

WET SNOW IS SWEEPING
  OVER THE RED-BERRY
  BUSH . . .
TWO SPARROWS CHIRPING
                    SHIKI

OVER AND OVER
  FROM MY BED
  I ASK MY NURSE:
NOW, HOW DEEP THE SNOW?
                    SHIKI

AT THIS DREARY INN
  A HOUND KEEPS
  WAILING . . . LIKE ME
LONELY IN THE RAIN?
                    BASHO

54

THE VERY PLANETS
   GLEAMING THROUGH
     ITS SILHOUETTE . . .
FROZEN WILLOW-TREE
          CHORA

EVERY SINGLE STAR
   IS QUIVERING NOW
     WITH LIGHT . . .
O HOW BITTER COLD
          TAIGI

BRIGHT SOUL OF WINTER . . .
   MOONLIGHT
   PUNCTUATED BY
PATTERING HAILSTONES
          GYODAI

BITTER WINTER WIND . . .
   WON'T IT BLOW
   RIGHT OFF THE SKY
THAT DAY-OLD CRESCENT?
          KAKEI

NOW AT DAWN THE TIDE
    FLOATS INCOMING
    LAYERS ON
OUR NIGHT-FROZEN COVE
                    SHIKI

POLISHING THE BUDDHA . . .
    AND WHY NOT
    MY PIPE AS WELL
FOR THE HOLIDAY?
                    ISSA

ON A RAINY DAY
    THE DRIPPING
    SCARECROWS SEEM LIKE
ORDINARY MEN
                    SEIBI

REMEMBERING
    THEIR PAINTED FACES . . .
    SHE UNWRAPPED
HER OLD PAIR OF DOLLS
                    BUSON

IT IS WARM TODAY . . .
  BUT I THINK
  I FEEL THE CHILL
OF THAT WINTER SUN
            ONITSURA

CHILDREN, COME ON OUT:
  CLATTERING
  ALONG THE LANE
SEE . . . IT'S HAILING PEARLS
            BASHO

ICY WINTER NIGHT . . .
  I UNFREEZE
  THE WRITING-BRUSH
WITH MY TWO GOOD TEETH
            BUSON

OUT OVER THE LAKE
  LONG COLD
    HOLLOW EMPTINESS . . .
A SOLITARY CROW
            SHIKI

THOSE TWO TIRED DOLLS
   IN THE CORNER
   THERE . . . AH YES
THEY ARE MAN AND WIFE
ISSA

SILLY HAILSTONES . . .
   FLEEING INTO
   MY FIREPLACE
FAST AS THEY CAN RUN
ISSA

IN ICY MOONLIGHT
   PIN-POINT-PATTERING
   PEBBLES
CRUNCHING UNDERFOOT
BUSON

COLD WINTER RAIN-LINES
   ARE LIFTED
   HORIZONTAL
BY THE HOWLING GALE
KYORAI

58

WITH THIS HAT BLOWN OFF
    THE STIFF-NECKED
    SCARECROW STANDS HERE
QUITE DISCOMFITED
                BUSON

ICY-WINTER NIGHT . . .
    PERHAPS THE WATER-
    BIRDS, LIKE ME,
ARE LAKESIDE HUDDLERS
                ROTSU

DARKENING SNOW-CLOUDS . . .
    OVER THIS WAITING
    LAKE AND LAND
BLACK BIRDS WHIMPERING
                OTOKUNI

BLUE-SHADOW-BOLTED . . .
    THE CASTLE GATE
    OF EDO
IN FROZEN MOONLIGHT
                KIKAKU

59

MY NEIGHBORS HATE ME . . .
   HEAR THEM BANG
   AND RATTLE PANS
IN THE ICY NIGHT

         BUSON

THAT SNOTTY URCHIN
   LEFT UNPICKED
   BY EITHER TEAM . . .
AH THE BITTER COLD!

         SHIKI

BEFORE THE BUDDHA
   EVEN GOOD SPARROWS
   BOW . . . PARENTS
AND CHILDREN BOTH

         ISSA

A HARSH-RASPING SAW
   MUSIC OF
   COLD POVERTY
IN WINTER MIDNIGHT

         BUSON

YEAR-END REVELLING . . .
  STILL IN PILGRIM'S
  CAPE MUST I
ROAM MY ENDLESS ROAD
          BASHO

SINCE DEAR BASHO DIED
  WHAT POEM-MAKER
  DARES TO WRITE
"YEAR-END REVELLING"?
          BUSON

DEATH-SONG

I WAS ALLOTTED
  TWO AUTUMNS MORE
  THAN AVERAGE MAN
THE HARVEST MOON
          SAIKAKU

DEATH-SONG

ON THE LAST LONG ROAD
  WHEN I FALL AND
  FAIL TO RISE . . .
I'LL BED WITH FLOWERS
          SORA